The Stolen Child

WB Yeats and Carl Jung
– Relationship, Belonging and Compassion
in Caring for Children in Care

Maurice Fenton

The Stolen Child

ISBN 978-0-9955509-0-2

Copyright ©2016 Maurice Fenton

Published by Empower Ireland Press

Printed in Ireland by Lettertec.

*This book is dedicated to my wife, Liz,
who stole my heart many years ago.
She has given me back far more than she took.*

*Also to the memory of my dear friends
MacDara and Hilary O'Siochrú
who were family to me 'when we were young'.*

He Wishes for the Clothes of Heaven

Had I the heavens' embroidered cloths,
Enwrought with golden and silver light,
The blue and the dim and the dark cloths
Of night and light and the half light,
I would spread the cloths under your feet:
But I, being poor, have only my dreams;
I have spread my dreams under your feet;
Tread softly because you tread on my dreams.

W. B. Yeats

Contents

The Stolen Child provides a powerful blend of personal narrative and academic commentary steeped in Irish folklore, history and poetry. The author offers a unique perspective on resilience, belonging, rejection and hope. This original and accessible writing is essential reading for all working in this field.

Dr Ray Arthur, Northumbria University, United Kingdom.

The word fabric occurs at intervals in this book. Indeed, the author himself has skillfully and provocatively woven his own analytical fabric to great effect. Opening with the poetry of Yeats, he imbues his narrative with it. He posits the absolute necessity to challenge the 'illusionary magic' of science as a cosy tool of bureaucracy that, despite grandiose claims, does little to put children in state care first.

Noel Howard, Treasurer, Social Care Ireland.

Prologue

This short book developed out of an email to Charles Shape of the goodenoughcaring.com Journal who was reviewing my book **Social Care and Child Welfare in Ireland: Integrating Residential Care, Leaving Care and Aftercare.** The review is available here: http://www.goodenoughcaring.com/the-journal/review-social-care-and-child-welfare-in-ireland-integrating-residential-care-leaving-care-and-after-care/

In this email, I sought to explain to Charles the reason why I choose a verse of poetry from W.B. Yeats's poem, The Stolen Child, for the dedications page of the book. Charles recommended that I expand on this email and he kindly published what resulted, titled, The Stolen Child, at: http://www.goodenoughcaring.com/the-journal/the-stolen-child/ together with a Stolen Child Part 2 at: http://www.goodenoughcaring.com/the-journal/the-stolen-child-part-two/

In this book, I have sought to partially retain this email structure to mark this connection to the goodenough-caring.com Journal as the original, personal, email to Charles became the basis from which this book evolved. Consequently, this book is both personal and academic. As is often the case, one thing led to another and the result is this book. I have found that writing for the goodenoughcaring.com Journal has been an excellent experiential learning process.

The verse of poetry on the dedications page of the book **Social Care and Child Welfare in Ireland: Integrating Residential Care, Leaving Care and Aftercare** reads:

The Stolen Child

Come away, O human child!
To the waters and the wild
With a faery, hand in hand,
For the world's more full of weeping
Than you can understand.

W.B. Yeats

Introduction

Dear Charles,

When you get to reading the book you may wonder why I chose the verse from W.B. Yeats's poem 'The Stolen Child' for the dedications page so I thought that I would give you a brief accounting as to why I chose it, to afford you insight into my thinking in matching this poem with this book.

I am no great aficionado of poetry, more the opposite in truth, but this poem resonates with the sense of loss I experience for those young people who I have known but who died whilst still involved with the care system, mostly whilst leaving care or shortly thereafter. The full poem reads:

Where dips the rocky highland
Of Sleuth Wood in the lake,
There lies a leafy island
Where flapping herons wake
The drowsy water rats;
There we've hid our faery vats,
Full of berries
And of reddest stolen cherries.
Come away, O human child!
To the waters and the wild

With a faery, hand in hand,
For the world's more full of weeping than you can
understand.
Where the wave of moonlight glosses
The dim gray sands with light,
Far off by furthest Rosses
We foot it all the night,
Weaving olden dances
Mingling hands and mingling glances
Till the moon has taken flight;
To and fro we leap
And chase the frothy bubbles,
While the world is full of troubles
And anxious in its sleep.

Come away, O human child!
To the waters and the wild
With a faery, hand in hand,
For the world's more full of weeping than you can
understand.
Where the wandering water gushes
From the hills above Glen-Car,
In pools among the rushes
That scarce could bathe a star,
We seek for slumbering trout
And whispering in their ears
Give them unquiet dreams;

Leaning softly out
From ferns that drop their tears
Over the young streams.
Come away, O human child!
To the waters and the wild
With a faery, hand in hand,
For the world's more full of weeping than you can
understand.

Away with us he's going,
The solemn-eyed:
He'll hear no more the lowing
Of the calves on the warm hillside
Or the kettle on the hob
Sing peace into his breast,
Or see the brown mice bob
Round and round the oatmeal chest.

For he comes, the human child,
To the waters and the wild
With a faery, hand in hand,
For the world's more full of weeping than he can
understand.

Yeats's poem speaks of children beguiled away into another realm by the faeries, as outlined in the notes and analysis of the poem below taken from the www.ireland-calling.com website:

'There were many stories about fairies snatching children away and although no one took such tales too seriously, they could still create fear and unease in the subconscious of rural people well into the 20th century. Yeats loved such stories and they provided a rich vein of material for his early writing. The Stolen Child was first published in Irish Monthly in 1896. It also appeared in Yeats' first collection of Poems, Crossways, which was published in 1889.

The poem is called The Stolen Child but the fairies beguile the boy into coming with them rather than actually steal him. They begin by offering food with "vats full of berries and of reddest stolen cherries". This may seem commonplace today but rich fruits would have been a luxury in 19th century Ireland. The fact that the cherries are stolen also conjures up the idea of "forbidden fruit" which adds to the sense of temptation. The fairies also beguile him with stories of dancing and merriment, and of mischief such as playing tricks on slumbering trout. They also play on the young boy's fear, telling him that "the world's fuller of weeping than you can understand". This point is repeated in a four-line chorus at the end of each verse. It has a chanted, hypnotic rhythm which adds to the sense that the boy is being beguiled.

Having enticed the boy away in the final verse, the fairies contrast the familiar domestic sights he's leaving such as the kettle boiling on the hob, with the "waters and the wild" that will be his new home. Although the boy goes voluntarily, he is still stolen in the sense that he has been bewitched by the fairies' chanting. The boy is unhurt but the reader is still left with a sense of unease, loss and foreboding.

The Stolen Child references actual places in Ireland

The Stolen Child is set in Yeats' native Co Sligo and in nearby Leitrim. Sleuth Wood is in Sligo where it is also known as Slish Wood. It comes from the Irish word, sliu, which means a slope or incline. Sleuth Wood therefore literary means 'sloping wood'. Rosses is on the coast of Sligo. It was a popular seaside destination for the Yeats family. Local folklore suggested it was also a popular haunt for fairies. Glencar Waterfall is in Co Leitrim, just across the border from Sligo.'

The plot of the poem has been identified by many as a metaphor for the return to innocence, which is characterised by Yeats as childhood. The world of 'fantasy' which Yeats creates contrasts sharply with the real world, a world which Yeats was said to have experienced dissatisfaction with. A dissatisfaction that might be said to be no more evidenced than in his relationship with the love of his life, Maud Gonne.

Glencar waterfall, which features prominently in 'The Stolen Child', is pictured on the front cover of this book with 'bare' Benbulben, under which Yeats is buried, featuring on the back cover. His grave is marked by a plain headstone with the following self-composed epitaph:

Cast a cold eye

On life, on death.

Horseman, pass by!

Chapter 1 – Belonging

So the faeries beguile or entice the child into willingly going away with them and escaping a *'world that's full of troubles and anxious in its sleep'* by employing the allure of adventure, sweet berries and camaraderie but, in reality, the children are stolen from this world never to *'hear the kettle on the hob again'*. I have had the folklore of faeries instilled in me since childhood, both in school and culturally, in Ireland. I acquired a deep-seated appreciation for the cultural meaning-making role of the stories of faeries and 'other world' entities within our rich tradition of folklore that still today is embedded in the psyche of us Irish folk wherever we may be. We have a common expression here in Ireland for someone who is not paying full attention to something or on the same page as others on certain matters; we say that they are 'away with the faeries' meaning that they are in a world of their own or, for example, daydreaming. This, I believe, demonstrates that the cultural acceptance of the concept of faeries is a widespread phenomenon here in Ireland and likely further afield amongst other races also. Rationally I may know some things are facts and others myths but still I know also that there is more to this world than 'meets the eye' or lies beyond perception, just as there is the conscious, subconscious and unconscious mind.

We are very fortunate here in Ireland to have a landscape dotted with faerie forts and earth rings with tress, often whitethorn or oak, growing in the middle. To this day few farmers will tamper with these structures or cut these trees because of either respect for our shared cultural heritage or for fear of upsetting the faeries and suffering the consequences of their wrath; for these Irish faeries, including *banshees, dullahans, merrows, grogochs, pookas, changelings* and *leprechauns*, are a mischievous lot, possessed of dark and oftentimes malevolent natures.

I take pride in passing this lore to my children, the younger ones, now marinating in the luscious, but fleeting, certitude of adolescence deride my stories of faeries and the like but all the while they are absorbing these stories which I know they too will, in due course, pass on to their children. This, I am conscious, is key to our identity formation and I am keen to pass on to my children what was passed on to me. Just as I know they will pass this on so also I know that much of the work undertaken by me, and countless other social care workers, with children in care may not 'evidence' itself by bearing visible fruit until long after we have parted company. I do, however, wonder how children in care are impacted by the fragmentation to their identity formation through deficits in areas such as this. It is partly the personal narrative that connects us to each other and creates a sense of belonging. Eric Erikson (1952) identified that stable identities were a deterrent to the generation of anxieties with respect to the future and are therefore linked to ontological security, an issue we shall return to in chapter five. As Bruce Perry has said: "*Without a life story, a child is adrift, disconnected and vulnerable.*" (Perry in Rose, 2012:16)

So Yeats's poem, immersed as it is in this lore of faeries and the folklore of rural Ireland, resonates deeply within me. It is a poem I can understand. It also helps that this poem has been beautifully put to song with a haunting melody by the Waterboys and available here:
https://www.youtube.com/watch?v=vOzbqY1ABwQ

But it's not the folklore aspect of this poem alone that resonates with me; it is also pain, loss and sadness that effects this resonance. I lost my father at age 12 and it took many years for me to come to terms with this loss. He was stolen from me and also from the promise of his own life that he had worked hard to create. Yet he still lives within me, partly through the stories and cultural heritage he passed on to me and also though my undying connection to him. To this day he plays a key role in shaping my identity and these stories connected me to my cultural heritage thus affording me a deep sense of belonging. I connected with my tribe across generations, which placed the 'me' within the 'we', w(m)e, thereby strengthening my sense of identity, the me. The engendering of a sense of belonging for children in care is, I believe, one of the core challenges of social care practice and no more so than for those unaccompanied children in care.

I have always been struck by the line *'for the world' more full of weeping than you can understand* which speaks to me of immense sadness and hurt which I can identify with through my own experience of the loss of my father. This loss is a personal experience I recognise as a prior wounding event as theorised by Carl Jung in his concept of the 'wounded healer'. This was my wounding event which I believe rather than rendering me a flawed professional has enabled me to attune better to those I care for as Jackson (2001) outlines with regard to 'wounded healers'.

This line of poetry also speaks to my curiosity as to the other aspects, elements and/or dimensions of this world, including those within the professional domain, which may not 'meet the eye', for as Einstein said *'not all that matters can be counted'*. I find that in my direct practice I am often a seeker of the abridged why as I must live in the moment with the children and young people I am caring for often with little time to ponder when pressed to make daily-life event decisions. Whereas, when time allows, I seek via critically reflective processes the deeper meanings that often reside deeply buried beneath layers of feelings, emotions and behaviours. Such reflective processes afford the added advantage that learning can be achieve via turning hindsight into foresight in order to reveal insight and thereby practice is improved. This personal and professional curiosity is an attribute I value highly and one I hope I retain in my future practice as, I am conscious, it also means I am more likely to afford each individual I encounter genuine respect by not pre-judging them based on potentially erroneous pre-conceptions. This avoidance of judgment is, I believe, more likely to be the case as curiosity induces thinking and as Jung has said *'thinking is difficult, that's why most people judge'.*

I introduce the personal to this professional communication as I feel that this is appropriate and is in line with my argument within the book with regard to the place of the private, personal and professional aspects of self in our practice. Also, I believe that much of the professional self is also the personal self and, of course, both are political - and in today's globalised world the professional, the individual and the political are also universal.

My experience working with children and young people, predominately in residential care over the past 20 something years, causes me to see little distinction between a young person who dies by suicide or one who dies by drug or alcohol overdose, as so many do. It is shocking that, in Ireland, 25% of all deaths from non-natural causes, including suicide, of children and young people in care and aftercare over a 23-year age span, occur within one year, at age 18. Equally shocking is the fact that for young people in aftercare non-natural deaths outnumber natural deaths by a ratio of 5:1 (Fenton, 2015). These tragic statistics demonstrate that it is the stress and lack of preparation and thereafter support for young people who have left care at 18 that is the major cause of these deaths. Loneliness and stress are hidden malignant realities for many of these young people, the cause of much self-sabotaging behaviour.

Our current care system means that those who most need support are the ones least likely to receive support as they are less likely to engage in education or training and are therefore deemed ineligible for access to meaningful aftercare support. When they most need care and support, at age 18, it is not available to them profoundly reinforcing the experiencing of prior abandonment by family and compounded by current rejection by, and exclusion from, society. This is a prime example of an 'inverse care law'.

These young people who die by overdose have often experienced such alienation that they seek the only solace or escape from a *'world that's full of troubles'* they can find is in drink and/or drugs and, in my experience, their deaths are often closely linked to being at a very low ebb and filled with hopelessness and despair; so I see little distinction between such a death or suicide. Both are born of unbearable pain, hopelessness and despair. The sheer waste of a life that should have been full of promise but instead is full of pain is heart-breaking. I think Yeats captured this in his line *'for the world's more full of weeping than you can understand'* as who could 'understand' such pain sufficiently that they can live with it and lead a fulfilling life! Yet, many in fact do, including those care leavers who may have experienced the least successful care biographies, yet struggle on, surviving as best they can. They may remain marginalised by, and excluded from society, yet remarkably many go on to overcome this and lead fulfilling lives. This is true resilience and I am inspired by the capacity of those who overcome such adversity. I like to think that some of their resilience has rubbed off on me vicariously, counterbalancing the vicarious trauma and vicarious vulnerability I know I have also experienced (Fenton, 2015).

But not all have such fortitude, personality characteristics, social and economic support networks or perhaps good fortune. Those young people who tragically die in this transition, I believe, have had the promise of their future lives stolen. Stolen from them and us and we, as a society, are the poorer for it. Stolen first by abuse, neglect and/or abandonment, most often within their families, and then the eradication of their hope through repeated broken promises and failure to adequately care for them when removed from these families and placed in out-of-home care settings. Followed then by the lack of support and opportunity after care has (re)abandoned them after they turn 18 years of age and finally by continuous rejection and stigmatisation in society.

"It's the children the world almost breaks who grow up to save it." Frank Warren

So for me at least, there is a strong sense of connection between Yeats's stolen child beguiled away by the faeries and these young people beguiled away by drink and/or drugs; both are vulnerable and are seduced by false promise, ultimately, and tragically, ending up stolen from this world. It is for these reasons that I chose this poem.

However, this choice, as so often happens when we make choices, opened a door through which I have chosen to enter and further explore the poetry of Yeats and its relevance to my work, which I shall return to after first considering the place of feelings and emotions in social care in more depth.

Whilst there have been many improvements within aftercare, particularly in the past decade or so, it is those at the margins that I most identify with as these are the ones I have known over the years while working in residential care and aftercare; those children and young people that are largely 'hidden from the public view' - out of sight and largely out of mind. It may be that I too find their pain vicariously unbearable and am, at times, affected by vicarious trauma but it is certainly true that I find the social injustice unacceptable. However, I won't seek to deny the professional and cognitive dissonance these feelings and emotions induce by attempting to intellectualise, theorise or rationalise them into acceptable or manageable frameworks in pursuit of the often misunderstood construct of 'being professional'. I have learned from the lengthy and painful process of coming to terms with the death of my father that the denial of feelings and emotions only brought more and greater pain into my life and that only by accepting, owning and staying with painful feelings and emotions was resolution to be found. Therefore, I recognise that to deny the feelings of dissonance in this case would also be to deny the injustice perpetrated on so many care leavers and prolong their pain.

"*To understand, and therefore to be able to help, another person requires a capacity for empathy: to stand momentarily in the other's shoes and experience their pain, using what one has learned as a guide as to how best to respond.*" (Obholzer and Roberts 1994:117)

Chapter 2 –
Feelings, Emotions and Objectivity

I believe that feelings and emotions are inalienable to genuinely caring for another human being and I agree with Nel Noddings (1996) who said that if a child does not feel they are being cared for they are being treated as an object. The risk of objectification is exacerbated within increasingly commodified and financially constrained systems wherein the social professions function. Political influence and the use of language are key drivers in such processes where, for example, people become labelled as clients or service users and recording and reporting mechanisms, largely geared towards the immaturely-conceived elimination of risk and the generation of statistical data, have become onerously and unhelpfully dominant within practice. Such statistical data repositions the individual 'troubled' child to becoming homogenised into groups labelled as 'troublesome' children. These 'troublesome' children, analogous to those care leavers who do not participate in education or training, then become identified as undeserving of access to the resources available for children which they so desperately need. In the language of commodification, they are perceived as representing poor ROI (return on investment).

Rather, resources which have, questionably, become identified as precious and therefore needing protection by economic circumstances and neoliberal dogma are made available to those deemed 'deserving'. Deserving, as they will more likely make tangible and recordable positive use of these resources, perhaps because they are deemed not yet to be so contaminated as to be beyond salvation (Ferguson, 2007). Through such processes further statistics are generated that paint a positive picture of a dysfunctional and inequitable care system evaluated within fiduciary rather than human paradigms. If, as Nelson Mandela said, a nation should be judged not by how it treats its highest citizens but by how it treats its lowest then applying the same rationale to our care and aftercare systems affords a less than complimentary picture and one contrary to that espoused by those who hold responsibility for developing and implementing these systems. A hallmark of true professionalism for those so tasked is the refusal to defend the indefensible.

"Due to the limited and shrinking availability of funds and the requirement to spend them efficiently to obtain maximum results (Mayhew, et al., 2005), assessment is considered necessary to identify those 'most vulnerable' or 'most at risk' and ensure only the 'most deserving' get access to assistance and support. Needs assessments are therefore fundamental

tools in policy making and implementation. They are considered 'objective' tools, but some have demonstrated that they are not unproblematic, but rather biased (Brown, 2012; Olivier de Sardan, 2005:85). These processes of identification and assessment, instead of overcoming social inequalities, often build on, and reproduce, them (Wedal et al., 2005:36)." (Melrose and Pearce, 2013:140)

I believe the reification of that fabled state labelled 'objectivity' has the potential to lead to the compartmentalisation (or suppression) of bona-fide emotional responses and a denial of the reality that hurt can be a price of caring just as pain can be a price of love, as I found out with the loss of my father. Such prejudice favours those who may have no or limited experience of caring or who have practice experience but can no longer tolerate the emotional cost of caring. In a Bourdieusian* context the question is are those who write the rules for, or referee or coach (teach), 'the game' (the *field* of social care/ work) predominately those who are no longer capable of

---

*Pierre Bourdieu (1930-2002) was an influential French sociologist and intellectual who wrote extensively on aspects of power and its reproduction in society. Cultural capital, habitus and field are key constructs he theorised.

the feelings that afford 'a feel for the game' and if this is the case is the game then 'fixed' or rigged to validate and align with their agendas (via the prejudicial reproduction of specific *habitus* by practitioners) which reinforce their *capitals*, at the expense of authentic relational caring?

Could it be that there is a connection here between the demotion of the relevance of feelings and emotions and the apparent ambivalence exhibited by many professionals with regard to child and adolescent mental health issues?

Sometimes it is as fundamental as right and wrong and our feelings and emotional responses can play a key role in assisting with the differentiation of this distinction (Fenton, 2015a). These feelings and emotions can also inform other critical distinctions such as between instinct and intuition, where, in my personal experience, intuition has proven to be far more trustworthy and contextually valid than instinct.

Supposed facts and evidence have a propensity to change over time, their interpretation being influenced by new knowledge as in the case of DNA evidence in criminal proceedings when executed convicts have been exonerated posthumously. Clearly, the paramountcy of context must always be acknowledged, particularly in the social professions, and context is, after all, ever changing.

Then, there are those times when the penny drops and we see the facts that have been staring us in the face, hidden as Holohan (2011) put it *'In Plain Sight'*, but which we had failed to recognise. Therefore, with regard to facts and evidence, there are always unknown facts that may become known at an unknown time as highlighted by Donald Rumsfeld when he said: *'there are known knowns, known unknowns and unknown unknowns'*. This, of course, means that our factual knowledge is incomplete and ever changing and therefore relying solely on, alleged, facts and evidence to determine approaches and eligibility to, as well as quality of, care is patently flawed. Of course, I recognise that feelings can and frequently do change, as it must be noted does context, yet we must also acknowledge that some feelings such as the bonds of affection often last, unchanged, a lifetime. We would do well to acknowledge the importance currently being accorded to Emotional Intelligence and Competence (Morrison, 2007; Ingram, 2013; University of East Anglia, 2016) and social skills (Deming, 2015) within many professions where Emotional Quotient (EQ) is increasingly becoming valued above Intelligence Quotient (IQ). This is especially the case when it comes to leadership (Thompson, 2015).

Emotional Intelligence, first identified by the psychologists Salovey and Mayer in 1990, was popularised in the mid-1990s by Daniel Goleman. Although not all agree with his model, most now agree that Emotional Intelligence exists and is a factor in personal success and also that it can be improved. Goleman defined it as:

"Understanding one's own feelings, empathy for the feelings of others and the regulation of emotion in a way that enhances life."

Paradoxically, in professions founded on relationships, social care/work, the techno-rationale remains privileged despite the recognition afforded to the importance of Emotional Competence (Howe, 2008). Rather than seeing emotions as solely clouding judgement or distorting logic, an oft cited claim of those professionals who no longer have a 'feel for the game', emotional competence validates the inclusion of emotionally-informed information into decision making processes as a valuable means of informing decision making. In the social professions scientific approaches amenable to quantification remain reified partly based on the false premise that they are unchanging and allegedly devoid of bias when clearly this is not the case in either regard given the paramountcy of context and the fact that the dismissal of feelings and emotions is itself a bias.

"The capacity to be in touch with the client's feelings is related to the worker's ability to acknowledge his or her own. Before a worker can understand the power of emotion in the life of the client, it is necessary to discover its importance in the worker's own experience." (Shulman, 1999:156)

Furthermore, whilst essential for the expression of empathy with another human being there are also the actions that these feelings and emotions may inspire that must be appreciated. Here, it is not the feelings or emotions themselves that are the most important factor, it is actions that count. But, if we deny the feelings and emotions in the first instance then we also deny the potential for the sorely needed actions they may prompt. Actions that, for example, may be essential to improve our current incongruent system of care, which results in such tragic and unconscionable outcomes for too many care leavers. I believe that the lack of recognition for the importance of feelings and emotions also tends to pathologise the righteous place of passion in social care and I am proud to say I love my profession. I also believe that the role of feelings and emotions (and intuition) as well as that of dialogue within the process of turning theory into practice (praxis) requires re-evaluation and re-positioning within the hierarchy of relevance in the social professions (Trevithick, 2014).

"The intuitive mind is a sacred gift and the rational mind is a faithful servant. We have created a society that honors the servant and has forgotten the gift." Albert Einstein

Whilst acknowledging that the word trauma is, questionably, being increasingly used to describe an ever widening array of events, circumstances and conditions in the 21st century, as are the words therapeutic and resilience, with Sehgal (2015) describing resilience as *"a word that is somehow so conveniently vacant that it manages to be profound and profoundly hollow"*, nonetheless it is true to say that we have all experienced varying degrees of trauma. We have, for example, all experienced bereavement and loss, and each of us deals with traumas differently. There are those professionals who maintain that all trauma can be processed into something else, perhaps a benign memory or some other construct couched in euphemistic terminology that need no longer causes emotional distress or unduly influence our thinking. This, I suspect, may afford a sense of (professional) superiority by affording the person the veneer of being uninfluenced by emotional responses and therefore of being 'objective'. However, this can also place unrealistic expectations, and therefore feelings of failure and weakness, on many who are struggling with such loss and other forms of trauma just as the obsession with resilience in social care/work/policy can cause similar negative experiences, and worse, for those who fail to exhibit the desired outcomes attributed to resilient people. For example, it is known that there is a disturbing frequency of early life bereavement among young adults in conflict with the law. Vaswani (2008) collected data from 33 young prisoners, aged 16-20 years, and found that 91% had experienced at least one such bereavement (T2A, 2015:18). Such undesirable societal consequences of trauma cause me to wonder if neoliberalism has merely re-framed this concept of a phenomenon, resilience, which I accept does exist but likely not in this form, to further its pernicious and procrustean agendas?

Here, this neoliberally defined form of resilience is seen as a potential antibiotic or super-drug targeted at dealing with the symptoms of the underlying diseases thereby diverting attention from where it is most needed i.e. dealing with the actual diseases of neglect, poverty, social exclusion, abuse and community deprivation (Fenton, 2015). Those who fail to respond favourably to this antibiotic are then deemed irresponsible due to non-successful participation in the dispensation programmes involving this antibiotic and therefore deemed to be solely responsible for their plights and no longer 'deserving' of state support, regardless of their life circumstances.

Neoliberalism presents parallels with Darwinism but with a hyper-acceleration of processes analogous to those Darwin theorised. Here, it is the survival of the fittest (financially), the winners or 'the deserving', to the detriment of the less fortunate, the losers or 'the undeserving', with the markets (the mother (nature)) nurturing the former at the expense of the latter. This is a most artificial form of *un*natural selection. But is this a society we would wish for our children?

"One of the most pernicious aspects of market individualism is its suggestion that individuals have within them the power to lift themselves out of all hardships, and that those who do not exercise this power deserve to be the victims, only surviving at the mercy of those who use their power to the full. Capricious fortune may endow some of us with better initial conditions than others to live a fulfilling life, but it can just as easily throw us into tragic circumstances. It is the deep seated feeling that we need to care for other, just as we need others to care for us, that lies at the heart of human solidarity. When this feeling is dismissed as unworthy of competitive market heroes, it threatens to undermine the possibility of communal existence." (Tam,1998:129-130)

I see resilience all around me in the children and young people I meet both in care and after they have left care. They have experienced the worst of adverse childhood events (ACEs) yet they strive to overcome these traumas and in my experience most often want no more than to grow into independent and happy adults no different than others in society; the very society that has allowed these traumas to befall them in the first place and may also be intolerant of them as children in care. Yes, some days some may struggle with this burden and succumb to negativity or self-sabotaging behaviours but I am always mindful of just what they are dealing with and am inspired by their resilience. They, and others like them, are to me what true resilience is.

Chapter 3 –
Compassion, Pain, Resilience and Recovery

What I believe is notably absent from the aforementioned processes of addressing trauma is compassion, both in how we approach and understand others and also ourselves (Neff, 2015). It is the latter form of compassion that I have found requires constant conscious cultivation as this was not within my personal characteristics profile on entering social care to the same extent that compassion for others was. Yes, we must understand our reactions and responses to the pain of others and ensure we recognise and differentiate our needs from the others' needs, but then these needs need not be mutually exclusively met. Some of the best social care workers I have worked with over the years have managed to skilfully and appropriately combine both and in this process develop meaningful relationships with difficult to reach young people.

Participating professionally in such relationships requires critical (self) reflection and an appreciation of the potential for processes of transference and counter-transference with personal therapeutic process, at times, necessary on the part of the professional. However, whilst addressing such personal dynamics may at times be essential it is important to recognise that often there is no quick fix, despite the promises of some therapies.

Time is also essential, though of itself time does not heal. Time affords opportunity for the acquisition of positive experiences of what works for the individual, as well as that which doesn't. Time then allows the space for the re-authoring of internalised blueprints for how the inner-self relates and responds to the external world, thus enabling change to permeate through all levels of consciousness. Just as courage is not contingent on the absence of fear, equally recovery is not contingent on the absence of pain or emotional distress. Rather, it is the recovery of the ability to live life fully and authentically by experiencing the complete spectrum of human feelings and emotions including love and joy as well as pain. Yes, in many cases recovery can include the transformation of painful memories into less painful or distressing memories which do not evoke the same emotional responses and possible emotional flooding as previously. However, recovery can also be seen to be founded on the ability to regulate, or to accommodate and learn to live with, rather than transform or eliminate painful memories and emotions confirming that for many, trauma is both an event and an experience.

Such a perspective is advocated by researchers, most notably Calhoun & Tedeschi (2013) who have identified a potential outcome to trauma they have termed PostTraumatic Growth. This, they posit, is the experience of positive growth that individuals experience as a result of their struggle with a traumatic event(s). The paradox here is that the individual is rendered more vulnerable, yet stronger. In reality they are stronger having grown from the traumatic experience and no longer live in fear of bad things happening to them, as bad things have happened to them and they have survived. They have become, partially at least, inoculated against the fear of risk so pervasive in today's society as posited by the like of the sociologists Ulrich Beck and Frank Furedi. This, then, poses the question of whether this is not resilience by another name? and if it is, then this clearly reinforces the previously made point that it is Emotional Quotient rather than Intellectual Quotient that can be most beneficial to human functioning in today's complex interconnected world particularly with regard to the development of personal resilience (Van Rooy and Viswesvaran 2004; Schneider *et al.*, 2013).

"PostTraumatic Growth is not necessarily an experience that leads people to feel less pain from tragedies they have experienced, nor does it necessarily lead to an increase in positive emotion." (Calhoun & Tedeschi, 2013:21)

However, there is a third form of quotient which sits alongside IQ and EQ that warrants inclusion when contemplating resilience, and no more so than with regard to children in care all of who have experience of having to deal with adverse childhood events. This is Adversity Quotient (AQ), a concept first identified by Stoltz (1997). Stoltz defines AQ as 'the capacity of the person to deal with the adversities of his life. As such, it is the science of human resilience'. AQ is founded in three branches of science: psychoneuroimmunology, neurophysiology and cognitive psychology.

Psychoneuroimmunology is a field in science that examines the mind-body relationship. In essence, it studies the relationship between what one thinks and feels and what goes on in the body. How do thoughts and feelings affect the body and its overall health?

Neurophysiology is a field in science that focuses on the brain. It studies how the brain learns and functions. How are habits formed and what must occur to change habits once they are established?

Cognitive Psychology is the most popular aspect of psychology focusing on the relationships between thoughts and feelings associated with one's mental health. While there are many aspects to cognitive psychology, of particular importance to AQ is the research examining the human need for control or mastery over one's life.

Adversity Quotient encompasses four dimensions which measures the AQ of an individual. They are Control – the perceived control over adversity, Ownership – the perceived ownership over the outcomes of adversity, Reach – how far the adversity reaches or gets into the areas of a persons' life, and Endurance – this is linked to the perceived duration of the adversity. These four dimensions are embodied in the acronym C.O.R.E.

Stoltz developed an assessment instrument, a scientif-ically-grounded tool, he called the Adversity Response Profile (ARP). This, Stoltz maintains, is a valid predictor of one's success, stress-threshold, performance, risk-taking, capacity for change, productivity, perseverance, improve-ment, energy, and health.

So whilst IQ has traditionally been the focus of much research in predicting an individual's potential for success with EQ having become the focus of much similar research in recent decades, and undoubtedly these are important factor in predicting an individual's potential to succeed in life, they alone do not address the question of why some people react positively in the face of adversity and overcome hardship where others fail? Here, it is important to recognize that resilience only *"surfaces in the face of hardship"* (Hawley, 2000:102) and does not refer to positive adaption in general so, clearly, consideration of an individual's potential to respond positively to adversity is critical to predicting their resilience. Consequently, it would appear that it is IQ, EQ and also AQ that require consideration when considering an individual's potential for developing resilience; the caveat being that whilst there exists a significant body of research conducted on AQ with regard to specific domains there is as yet to be similar body of research on the concept of AQ and with regard to children in care and also that there are factors external to the individual that must also be considered when contemplating resilience as outlined in the social ecology model of resilience (Ungar, 2012). Further research into this area may illuminate the potential for a balancing of known deficits in specific quotients (Rutter, 1999) with high scores in AQ with regard to children in care. They are, after all else is said and done, highly experienced in being faced with adversity.

With regard to the aforementioned dynamics of dealing with trauma, it is notable that the acceptance of vulnerability, together with embracing risk, trusting feelings, the avoidance of assumptions and pre-judgment as well as being open to new experiences constitute the characteristics which Carl Rogers (1965) identified as being present in a '*the fully functioning person*'.

Trauma can cause us to seek to avoid the re-experiencing of pain we associate with the traumatic experience but this can be at the cost of experiencing joy in our lives. Many traumas occur within our relationships with other people and therefore it can be our current relationships which are negatively impacted by such traumas and, in reality, it is these very current relationships which offer us the most viable pathways to recovery.

"*A particular strength of this approach (relational) is to restore trust in other human beings where it has been lost, or to provide a place to work though other relationship problems, including problems arising from their environment (Wilson, 2000, p. 350).*" (Cited in Trevithick, 2003:168)

Yeats portrays how the allure of escape from a '*world more full of weeping than you can understand*' can precipitate becoming stolen from this world and all its everyday and ordinary experiences. It is these ordinary experiences, such as '*the lowing of the calves on the warm hillside,*' that are often where joy and meaning are to be found. The significance Yeats attaches to nature and the simple things in life is a theme running through much his poetry. Perhaps this explains its widespread popularity as it connects the reader to that most powerful human collective and universal condition, the experiencing and re-experiencing of feelings and emotions, especially those most-meaningful of feelings and emotions associated with childhood.

For my part, I find that when I stop and take in the beauty of the nature I am removed from my troubles and connected to a world much greater than myself. A world, free from human obligation, within that most beautiful wildness that is all around me in the landscape of Ireland. I am then, somewhat paradoxically as I reconnect with humanity but across generations and therefore without everyday obligation, often reminded that this is the landscape that my ancestors beheld and my children and their children will behold, it was here before me and will be here after I am gone. The paradox here is that it is the disconnection which facilitates the enhanced (re)connection. I know then that I am but passing through and am truly privileged to live in such a beautiful place and, for however flawed we Irish may be this is 'our' flaw, part of what Yeats termed our '*indomitable Irishery*' and I am proud to say that I love my country. By becoming mindful of this I am then reminded how fortunate I am to be surrounded by love in my life; love of my work, love of where I live and the love of my family.

Realising this I may then appreciate just how privileged I am to be able through my work to try to make a difference for hurt children and young people who may be struggling to build such lives, just as I struggled following the death of my father and the perceived loss of his love. Then, of course, I lose this connection, succumbing to the inescapable human condition whereby that which is extraordinary becomes perceived as ordinary and I again become caught up in the day-to-day struggles of work and life. But then (mother) nature is, like Winnicott's 'good-enough parent', more often than not there when needed.

With regard to the importance of pain to human development I must state that I derive little or no pleasure or comfort from pain. However, I recognise the existential importance of pain not the least due to recognising that the experiencing of painful feelings such as guilt as essential for healthy moral development and social functioning. Also, within the context of this consideration of childhood and adolescence it must be recognised that one of the core tasks of adolescence is the struggle with unconsciously dealing with the painful existential injustices of life. Injustices such as the inevitability of death or the absence of guarantees in life, which generate an angst for the adolescent. This angst is then further fuelled by the increasing awareness of the fallibility of adults with the recognition that one's parents have 'feet of clay' and cannot shield the adolescent from the mortality of life and the reality that ultimately life is often not fair. The previously-noted certitude of adolescence is likely linked to this recognition of the fallibility of adults but this certitude is doomed to be short-lived as the adolescent emerges into adulthood and whilst taking on the robes of responsibility and independence of adulthood also takes on the fallibility previously identified in adults. The certitude lives, much like a caterpillar, within the all too brief window of transition somewhere between adolescence and adulthood, which, although protracting in recent decades (Arnett, 2007) remains a short life-stage in terms of duration comparative to adulthood.

Whilst recognising that adolescence angst does indeed exist, such a conception of adolescence also challenges the commonly held view of adolescence as a time of storm and upheaval as the certitude acts to counter-balances the angst. Perhaps this is one of its purposes and if so it ought well to be embraced by parent and carers for its critical role rather than dismissed, as it often may be, as immaturity and naïve arrogance.

This, then, brings to mind the work of another famous poet, Dylan Thomas, two of whose poems can be said to support some of the aforementioned arguments, albeit the poems in question were not written with adolescents in mind. Employing the poetic lense of these two poems, "And Death Shall Have No Dominion' and 'Do Not Go Gentle Into That Good Night', it can be argued that for the adolescent 'death has little or no dominion' as they embrace risk-taking in ways that challenge our adult judgement and, at times, apparently with less than due consideration for their mortality, living, as they tend to do, in the moment. Yet, once the adolescent accepts their mortality, which as we have seen is a pre-requisite to becoming 'adult', they begin the inexorable, compromise-laden journey, circuitous and undulating, towards death's embrace. "Do not go gentle into that good night' was written for Thomas's aged and dying father and is said by many to be an inspirational call to embrace life and 'rage' against inevitable death by living life to the fullest. Two immortal lines from this poem about death are:

> *Do not go gentle into that good night,*
> *Rage, rage against the dying of the light.*

However, this poem might equally be said to apply to the adolescent who also 'rages against the dying of the light' with non-conforming and, at times, ungentle behaviours which contest adult ways and therefore the acceptance of death's dominion. The adolescent can, in this context, be seen to be the champion of the human spirit rejecting compromise and defying the fear of death. This fear of death can be said to induce a deleterious impact on the quality of our adult lives where we endure 'death by a 1,000 cuts' - of sensible compromise. In our adult minds the adolescent is, above all else, synonymous with rebellion and is this not but an expression of rage, or passion, but in this context a righteous rage? Thus, Thomas's immortal words might equally apply to the adolescent for if they do not accept death's dominion then neither will the adult coming after them go gently into that good night. That righteous spirit of rage, where emotional responses and reactions are to the fore, would then be more prominent throughout our life spans and would we not then lead more fulfilling and lived lives with fewer regrets? Perhaps our sense of adult identity threatened by the adolescent is in fact a sense of dissatisfaction with ourselves for compromising and not being all that we could have become, including compromising on fully experiencing our own adolescence (Winnicott *et al.,* 1984)?

Such a consideration of the adolescent, coupled with a recognition of the reality of intergenerational conflict and power differentials between adolescents and adults (Fenton, 2015), then brings to mind Yeats's beautiful poem cited at the beginning of this book, "He Wishes for the Clothes of Heaven".

> *But I, being poor, have only my dreams;*
> *I have spread my dreams under your feet;*
> *Tread softly because you tread on my dreams.*

However, lest the reader thinks I am naïvely romanticising the adolescent and am myself away with the faeries on this point there is another less noble perspective I will proffer, though on the process of adolescence rather than the adolescent. By employing the metaphor of Yeats's 'The Stolen Child' I contend that adolescence can also be seen as the thief of childhood. Here, the (innocent) child previously idealised by their parents has apparently been stolen and replaced by a *'changeling'*, full of bravado, at times, masquerading as certitude and prone to bouts of defiance and ambivalence towards their parents and adult ways. The paradox of adolescence is that the adolescent has become imbued with the entirely natural drive to search for identity and the irresistible allure of adulthood and independence but, as we have seen, the promised certitude of adulthood is short-lived as they incrementally become that which they formerly reprehended. They have been beguiled by the faeryesque thief that is adolescence with its false promises of adulthood and then, on achieving adulthood, long for the lost innocence and simpler times of childhood. This longing for simpler times is thematic throughout much of Yeats's poetry.

With regard to children in care these matter have accentuated meaning. Children in care have experienced a range of adverse childhood events including parental abandonment, neglect, physical, emotional, mental, sexual and spiritual assault and felt rejection. This threatens their sense of identity as referenced earlier and also triggers autonomic primal fear responses associated with parental abandonment which renders the infant vulnerable to imminent death. Such experiences generate what Laing (1973) termed 'ontological insecurity' and have been linked to the development of Post-Traumatic Stress (Smith, 1987). Ontology is that branch of science, philosophical or metaphysical, that considers the nature of being, becoming, existence or reality and also the basic categories of being and their relations. In essence, determining what things actually exist.

Giddens (1991) considered ontological issues from the perspective of ontological security. Ontological security has been defined both as the certainty that the world we live in is as it appears to be and also the certainty of belonging to, being part of, and being accepted by a determined group.

Giddens *(ibid)* posited, inter alia, that home-ownership may promote greater ontological security and that globalisation may generate ontological insecurity as to trust in others an individual first needs an assured collective identity, the certainty of being part of some group.

"A globalized world is for many a world devoid of certainty, of knowing what tomorrow holds. It's a world where many people feel intensified levels of insecurity as the life they once led is being contested and changed at the same time. Globalization challenges simple definitions of who we are and where we come from. A number of factors related to globalization seem to have increased the gaps between those who have reaped the benefits of the global markets and those who have been left behind." (Kinnvall, 2004:742)

Yeats's Ireland, a land of great beauty and character yet beset by troubles and hardships, can be seen in the light of ontological insecurity where its natives fought such hardship stoically, with indomitable spirit. Some of these hardships such as disease and premature death may be partly attributed by the populace to the mischievous faeries but in reality these hardships are mostly attributable to oppression and poverty. This ontological insecurity, exacerbated by transgenerational trauma linked to such tragedies as the Great Famine (1845-1849), might then explain the high drive to achieve home-ownership amongst Irish people with historically above average European rates of home-ownership in Ireland formerly very evident. This drive to achieve home ownership appears to be unique to Ireland unlike similar oppressed indigenous populations elsewhere in the world who may be afflicted by similar ontological insecurity or, is it that the Irish indigenous people achieved independent statehood? For a state celebrating its first 100-year anniversary in 2016, perhaps this drive to achieve home-ownership may also be seen in light of ontological evolution where the sense of ontological security may be evolving as part of the state's maturation.

More recently Cashmore and Paxman (2006) built on this ontological concept in exploring what they termed the sense of 'felt security' of children in care and aftercare. These are very important matters for caring for children in care as referenced in chapter two. This importance can be partly illuminated by attachment theory which identifies how the internal blueprints laid down in infancy and early childhood can shape the individual's life-course development and functioning. How we perceive the world and our sense of security and belonging within this world plays a pivotal role in determining how we interpret and interact with the world and the people within this world across our life-course.

Clearly a sense of belonging is central to ontological security and by extension a deficit in the sense of belonging is associated with ontological insecurity. If we accept Giddens's thesis we can see that children, young people and families who experience homelessness are vulnerable to experiencing high levels of ontological insecurity. We must also recognise that children taken from their families and entered into care are vulnerable to experiencing a sense of abandonment and displacement compounded, too often, with frequent moves within care (Coy, 2009). Additionally, we have seen that childhood trauma can exacerbate ontological insecurity, so it is clear that there is a link between childhood trauma and the current sense of belonging experienced by children and/or young people in terms of their ontological security profile. We need to be focused on addressing these matters in order to optimally meet the developmental needs of children and young people in care because just as secure attachment patterns are positive indicators of healthy functioning so ontological security can be seen as essential to healthy functioning and wellbeing.

Returning to the topic of pain and bring this brief exploration of this subject to a conclusion, I accept that pain, in all its forms, is something that must be accepted rather than denied if we are to grow to our fullest potential as human beings; balance is the key. As Jung said: *'there is no coming to consciousness other than through pain'*, whilst Fredrich Nietzsche before him famously said:

"You have the choice: either as little displeasure as possible, painlessness in brief ... or as much displeasure as possible as the price for the growth of an abundance of subtle pleasures and joys that have rarely been relished yet? If you decide for the former and desire to diminish and lower the level of human pain, you also have to diminish and lower the level of their capacity for joy."

So for now I will continue to come to terms with this dissonance of caring for and about these most marginalised and downtrodden young people utilising what I learned from the process of coming to terms with the dissonance caused by the death of my father. I have, after all, first-hand evidence of what has actually worked and, for me, there can be no more robust evidence than this – lived experience. Lived experience is, I believe, as true a 'gold standard' of research as the Random Control Test. It is my reality and I know my own truth. I neither need nor desire for scientifically-derived evidence to do my thinking for me, which is not to say I disregard such evidence, but rather that I synthesise it along with, amongst other things, personal and collective lived experience in order to inform my professional judgment and opinion.

The propensity for professionals to allow evidence, especially scientific and in-vogue evidence, to do their thinking for them, a form of confirmation bias but with elements of the Emperor's New Clothes Syndrome (Born, 2005), is brilliantly captured by Eileen Gambrill who has said: *"When we see a picture of the human brain we stop thinking."*

Chapter 4 – Poetry and Social Care

So now I shall address my newfound interest in the poetry of Yeats and its relevance to the practice of social care in more depth. I believe Yeats's poetry evidences the universality and endurance across time of the experiencing of feelings and emotions, what in academic terminology is termed the reliability, generalizability and replicability of research together with another bastion of academic discipline, academic rigor, evidenced in the linguistic structure of his work. His poetry is after all a form of research into the lived human experience composed 130 years ago yet still as relevant today as when he composed it. The more I learn through life experience and academic endeavours the more I see the truth espoused by Yeats, perhaps Ireland's foremost poet, and Einstein, perhaps the world's foremost scientist. Yeats, for his line in the Stolen Child *'For the world's more full of weeping Than you can understand'* and Einstein who said *'the more I learn the more I realise I don't know'*. Here, I find truth as these two positions unite the artistic and creative aspects of being human with the scientific domain thereby affording an epistemological common ground – epistemology being a branch of philosophy that investigates the theory of knowledge including the source, nature, methods and limits of human knowledge.

But I am not the first to make such connections. There exists a significant body of literature linking Yeats's interest in the supernatural or magic, to Jung's science of psychology (Hollis, 1973; Meihuizen, 1992; Olney, 1992). This body of literature identifies how they explored convergent themes, with Yeats in some instances first identifying topics which Jung later developed, though through common interest and perhaps synchronicity rather than imitation on Jung's part (Yeats, 1901; Snow, 2014). The chronology of this convergence lends credence to what could be described as a thought-provoking quip, namely that 'magic begat science'. Here, chemistry can be seen to have come from alchemy, astronomy from astrology, pharmacology from herbalism and engineering and physics from the study of nature with a view to understanding and mastering her ways. Coupled with this, if we consider the significance of the use of language in psychology, academia and research the question then arises as to what scope may exist for poetry to broaden existing qualitative research methodologies as it has broadened the field of personal therapy with the addition of poetic therapy? We are after all human, not omniscient, beings (though with the potential for magic which perhaps we call resilience (Masten, 2015)). In fact, many notable figures have written of magic with regard to psychology and social care including Sigmund Freud (1939) and Thom Garfat (2003).

Could it be that adults, and we social care practitioners are first and foremost adult human beings, are seeking magic in our lives? Perhaps we are seeking to re-connect with the lost enchantment and curiosity (or innocence p. 43) of childhood where faerie tales were our source of meaning making, hope and inspiration in a world full of wonderment (Bettleheim, 1975).

"Youth is happy because it has the ability to see beauty. Anyone who keeps the ability to see beauty never grows old."
Franz Kafka

If the practice of social care, where the relationship acts as a catalyst to transform hurt and alienation into connection and recovery, is a form of art rather than formulaically-prescribed actions on the part of the worker, as I believe it to be, then is this not the seeking of magic? For, what is art, the communication of alternate interpretations (meanings) induced by the manipulation of people, words, symbols, sounds and images, if not a form of magic? And is this meaning individually-ascribed by each observer or participant not but an impact on the consciousness of that person? This, then means that art and magic are both processes that endeavour to alter human consciousness (change thinking and awareness) and in this process potentially facilitate the transcendence of personal experience.

For my part, I do believe in magic, I do I do, to paraphrase Peter Pan. I have witnessed magic happen many times in social care, and I have been fortunate enough to have been an actor within some small number of these occasions. Occasions where children and young people have overcome apparently intractable adversity and transformed into healthy and happy people through the power of relationship with supportive adults, peers (Devine, 2004; Edmond, 2014) and family members. For me, the relationship is the magical fabric the envelops and interconnects social care. A fabric woven with many different threads, including, but not limited to, those of acceptance, compassion, empathy, understanding, a desire to make a difference, affinity, respect, kindness, strength, belonging, courage, transcendence, inspiration, love, connection, forgiveness, play, listening, empowerment, partnership, support, growth, patience, humour, collaboration, encouragement, solidarity, healing and teaching. A fabric of ever-changing pattern, and thus unamenable to formulaic reproduction as each is uniquely woven, bespokely-tailored to fit the needs of the individuals in each relationship. A fabric so powerful that it can hold the otherwise boundless pain and distress that these children and young people experience and also the anxiety of those caring for them. A fabric, the whole of which is greater than the sum of the individual threads.

Some I have met are master-weavers by their very nature whilst others, including myself, may by nature only possess a desire to make a difference and have to work hard at creating and nurturing the other ingredients and adjusting the patterns necessary to weave this fabric. Here experience and perseverance can be of great assistance but it is the retention of the motivation to make a difference that is essential. In the retention of this motivation I have found self-care is of paramount importance.

This magic of relationship cannot be conjured on command and we may not always recognise its magnitude whilst experiencing it yet when we are aware we are in its presence we can harness its transformational power. Thereafter, it is another of its magic properties that without having any longer to be in its presence we can continue to benefit from its power and we may become more skilled at replicating the process of its creation. It is invisible, unquantifiable and powerful largely beyond my comprehension, yet, thankfully, I have felt something of its power in both my personal and professional life.

I believe that the fallacy of the positivistic approach with its 'appliance of science' methodologies (Alasuutari *et al.*, 2008) is the belief that everything in this world can be understood and accounted for and therefore, by extension controlled. This is in reality but a form of illusionary magic (Stivers, 1999).

"An approach that is grounded in the belief that "I already know" is one that is immobilised and is oblivious to context and perspective, which in turn pigeonholes experiences, behaviours, objects and other people into existing categories. In other words, an individual's way of knowing predisposes a way of being and may obstruct learning". (Bellefeuille and Ricks, 2010:1237)

I also recognise that my lived experience is my truth and not everyone else's. But then, and as previously highlighted, we know that via processes such as globalisation that the 21st century individual, Yeats's human child, is more and more becoming connected by the strands of the increasingly digitised global webs of human inter-connectivity. Webs that bind us all in an increasingly interdependent state.

Yet this universality of human connection pre-dates mere technological developments of the 20th or early 21st century as evidenced within the concept of the 'collective consciousness' first theorised by Emile Durkheim in the 19th century and Jung's concept of the 'collective unconscious' both of which infer a binding of all human beings within some form of collective. Perhaps Yeats's faeries are representation of the collective unconsciousness of the Irish people made conscious, as Jung theorised, through dreams, feelings and intuition and then recorded and communicated via poetry and storytelling in the quest to give meaning to nature.

An example which seems appropriate to outline here is that of the Hungry Grass, something it appears is only spoken of in Ireland. Its origins appear to be located in times of great hardship and poverty which were not uncommon in Ireland pre 1900. It is said that if you were out in the mountains and you stepped on Hungry Grass and didn't immediately have some bread to eat, you would be overcome by an attack of hunger that would render you so weak that you would be prone to dropping from exhaustion with death following thereafter. Alternatively, you might make it off the mountain but your fate was sealed and you would waste away over the following days and weeks and ultimately die of starvation. Even non-superstitious locals would not venture into the mountains without a mouthful of bread in their pockets for fear of encountering this grass. The Hungry Grass was said to have come into being as a result of people eating a meal on the mountain and not leaving some bread for the faeries. The faeries would then place a curse on the spot where the meal was eaten without due tribute and respect paid to them and any mortal unwittingly stepping onto this Hungry Grass, which is said to be a type of tough and wiry grass, without some bread to hand was doomed. It is true that starvation, poverty and disease were not uncommon in those times and nor was the discovery of dead bodies in mountain wilderness. But still today, there are those who will not venture into the mountains without bread in their pockets.

Jung asserted that the human psyche is constituted of four basic functions: intuition, thinking, feeling and (physical) sensation and he, and Carl Rogers amongst others, placed great emphasis on intuition, which he defined as '*perception via the unconscious*'. The recognition of the role of the unconscious has always been central to the psychodynamic approach and notably in recent times the significance of the unconscious has been making somewhat of a resurgence in the social professions and the human sciences. This resurgence is being supported by, inter alia, recent neuroscientific advancements which demonstrate that, at most, merely 20% of our brain is engaged with conscious processes leaving the remaining 80% involved in what can then only be sub or unconscious processes. With the rapid development of communications and social media in the 21st century coupled with the equally rapidly advancing mergence of human biology with technology with, for example, biological computing, one has to wonder are we witnessing the emergence of a new form of collective consciousness? Could it be we are witnessing the emergence of a next generation collective consciousness where our individual neural pathways are becoming globally interconnected via digital pathways, and if so what might this mean for the evolution of humankind?

With regard to the role of the unconscious in caring for adolescents it must be acknowledged that the unconscious struggle to navigate permissiveness and control is another core challenge of adolescence and one requiring an appreciation by workers of the power dynamics at play. It is my belief, based on my practice experience, that control within residential care for adolescents is largely an illusion, and the higher up the management ladder one goes the more illusionary it becomes. Once we accept this and cease trying to achieve control through coercion or reward we become liberated to achieve what in fact we are seeking, a healthy environment where children's needs are therapeutically met by staff whose wellbeing is valued and promoted.

By giving away 'control' to both staff and young people through empowering and then motivating them, congruence is enhanced. People will, given the right resources within the right circumstances, most often choose to do the right thing and this is true of residential care services too. Thus, by not seeking to control others we are less likely to need to exercise control and this is the great paradox of our current risk management and control hegemonies: *by seeking to control that which we cannot control we actually diminish what we are seeking.*

If we do not meet the needs of adolescents for autonomy and self-determination by empowering them with age-appropriate levels of agency they will either comply with our directives under duress and therefore not internalise the changes we are seeking to teach/engender/impose or they will reject our authority and through their assertive and non-compliant behaviour take the legitimate sense of agency they seek. If neither of these scenarios unfold then there is the potential for them to seek to have these needs met elsewhere which can expose them to a host of harms which we, the professionals, can do little to ameliorate as we have lost their trust and with this any possibility to meaningfully engage with and assist them.

If we are to achieve positive outcomes for children in care we would be better employed to embrace risk and relinquish control within risk-tolerant relational-approaches to care that promote the agency and internal locus-of-control of the staff and young people. However, all our interventions with children and young people must fit within the framework of their evolving capacities (Lansdown, 2005) and this must also include acknowledging the need for intervention in the event of temporally diminishing capacities. We must be brave enough to embrace risk beyond our current thresholds but also be brave enough to be decisive when, and only when, absolutely needed. I have learnt that control, like love, we must brave enough to largely give away in order to regain, but then, this is not so surprising as both involve caring.

Mentoring has proven to be highly effective in engaging and sustaining relationships with adolescents, largely I believe, as the altered power differential made possible between mentor and mentee as opposed to that between professional social care worker (the expert) and client/ service user/young person (the novice) *'taps into the very essence of the adolescent process, with the unconscious struggle between authoritarian and anti-authoritarian parts of the maturing self'* (Obholzer and Roberts, 1994:133).

Thus, it is apparent that the unconscious plays a central role in human development and therefore in social care. It is also apparent that Yeats, the poet, and Jung, the scientist, were converging in their focus on realms beyond consciousness and matters that may not 'meet the eye'. This is not as surprising as it may at first appear when we consider the mechanics of the scientific research method, the principles and procedures for the systematic pursuit of knowledge i.e. the process by which science is conducted. The scientific method is based on three forms of reasoning, abductive, inductive and deductive, two of which are predicated on the hypothesising of the un-provable, or put another way that which 'does not meet the eye' or that which 'may count but cannot be counted'. Inductive reasoning, based on employing data revealed by observation, patterns and current knowledge, determines conclusions, known as conjecture and deemed to be probable rather than provable, whilst abductive reasoning may be said to provide the best explanation to what is otherwise un-provable. Deductive reasoning allows for logically certain conclusions to be identified which are derived from of an opening statement, known as a premise, which is assumed to be true. However, the veracity of the conclusions is only ever as true as the premise and the validity of the argument.

"*Science depends, not on the inductive accumulation of proofs, but on the methodological principle of doubt.*" (Giddens, 1991:21)

Ultimately, the only scientific certainty is uncertainty. Science is about finding the most reliable way of thinking at the present level of knowledge and therefore the very expression "scientifically proven" is a contradiction in terms (Rovelli, 2014). Proofs only exist in logic and mathematics and science is far from the purely objective discipline many may believe it to be with findings that are always open to the possibility of change (Kuhn, 1962).

"*Scientific knowledge is in perpetual evolution; it finds itself changed from one day to the next.*" Jean Piaget

However, lest the reader think that my argument is too tenuous and that I too have been seduced by mysticism and am myself, again, 'away with the faeries' I adduce, once again, that elder statesman of science and intellect, Albert Einstein, many of whose most famous theories are based on inductive and abductive reasoning:

"*There is no logical way to the discovery of these elemental laws. There is only the way of intuition, which is helped by a feeling for the order lying beyond the appearance.*"

Chapter 5 –
Relationship and Residential Child Care

There are many aspects of relationship in social care and to begin to draw this short book to a close I will briefly consider some of these. These will include relational and relationship-based practice where the workers' relationship with themselves is to the fore - given that each worker is themselves their most empowering and protective factor in their work. Here, self-awareness is critical to their understanding of how they are impacting on those they seek to have relationships with and also how they themselves are impacted by these relationships (Anglin, 2004).

Then there is the relationship between the worker and their colleagues - both within their workplace and employing organisations as well as professionals from other domains and organisations. Here, as we try to engender the value of respect in the children and young people we support, both for themselves and others, we must role model this respect for our colleagues through our actions and challenge the, at times, adversarial and defensive inter-professional communications that can occur. We must do this both so that the children in our care witness us as appropriate role models and not preaching one standard for them but practising another ourselves and also, to develop positive relationships and form collaborative alliances with our colleagues. This must be our *'Common Way of Being'*.

I have noticed over the years how I began to recognise other social care practitioners similar in their outlook to me - an outlook which, I suspect, mostly comes from similar values and shared experiences of success and failure in caring for children and young people. I found myself often citing a Gaelic expression - what is called a seanfhocal - a seanfhocal is Gaelic for an old wise expression or proverb. This seanfhocal states - *Aithníonn ciaróg ciaróg eile* - one hedgehog recognises another hedgehog – and it is likely readers of this book will be similar hedgehogs by virtue of your interest and shared recognition of the potential of relationship to unite the professions and as the primary medium for supporting and healing traumatised and vulnerable children.

"Whilst the ability to forge good interpersonal relationships is desirable, but often not essential for highly developed professions such as medicine and law, it is an absolute precondition of effective social work practice (Chu and Tsui, 2008; Chu et al., 2009; Proctor, 1982; Ward et al., 2010). Before all others, the core skill required by social work is the capacity to relate to others and their problems." (O'Leary *et al.*, 2013:137)

Then there is the relationship between children, childhood and society as well as intergenerational relationships where our current chronologically-defined conception of childhood is being challenged more and more by evidence from neuroscience and other fields. These findings tell us that a maturational and developmental understanding of childhood is more appropriate in the 21st century (Davis & Vander Stoep, 1997; Bentley, 2005). Within this form of relationship the worker has responsibility to represent and advocate for and with children and young people - and also to empower them to advocate for themselves - by promoting values of social justice, highlighting and challenging injustices and inequities that afflict children and young people today.

We now come to another form of relationship – that between worker and child. This is where care is given and healing happens. Children can only feel this care through a relationship with their care workers who, as Stein (2012) has said, are the face of the corporate parent. The effectiveness of any programme or strategy will be determined by the ability of the worker to skilfully implement such programmes or strategies through the medium of meaningful relationship and employing their professional judgement (Li & Julian, 2012). Yet in recent times performance indicators for professional excellence have been redefined as accountancy and managerial skills with a transfer of power from professionals to managers (Smith, 2009; Evetts, 2011). Our profession has been subverted by techno-rational paradigms and a foreign language of commerce - it has been commodified.

It is a cause of grave concern when the focus of the work increasingly shifts from relationships to bureaucratic tasks (Munro, 2011; Furnivall *et al.*, 2012) and we cannot forget it is precisely in the area of relationships with adults that many young people experience difficulties. Consequently, the relationship focus holds the potential for young people to address life-changing issues through the medium of a safe relationship with an appropriate adult thus enabling lost trust to be restored (Howe, 1998; Trevithick, 2003).

> *"We are broken*
> *within the context of relationships;*
> *and we are also healed*
> *within the scope of relationships."*
> *(Nadjiwan, 2010:1)*

Residential Care

Then there are the relationships between children within residential care - an area where there is much misunderstanding and where residential care can be erroneously critiqued, an issue I have addressed in some detail elsewhere (Fenton, 2015). In truth, poor residential care can indeed be a disservice to children and young people placed therein as unless the matching of young people in residence together is carefully managed there is the very real potential for unintended negative consequences where low risk young people are mixed together with those with high-risk profiles (Little *et al.*, 2005; Dodge *et al.*, 2006). These unintended consequences included a young person becoming impacted by the negative influence of other young people in residence with them and either taking on some of these negative behaviours or becoming the victim of these behaviours directly impacting on them (Whitteker, *et al.*, 2015).

In my experience allied professionals can sometimes become frustrated with children's residential centres not admitting a child or young person who these professionals may desperately need placing in a place of safety, especially when no other placement is immediately available. Very often there is no other placement available as residential care is used as a placement of last resort (Schofield *et al.*, 2016), meaning that other forms of care have first been tried and only when these have failed, and often repeatedly, is residential care then considered. What this means is that the harm to these children and young people has been compounded by these multiple placement breakdowns (Coy, 2008) and the ability of any service or professional to successfully meet their needs decreased. Residential care is then expected to deal with what cannot be dealt with anywhere else which encompasses a vast range of trauma and pain-related needs and behaviours with known high-levels of mental-health conditions, often when the opportunity to successfully intervene has been previously, and repeatedly, missed. This of course poses the bona fide question as to what would happen to these children and young people were residential care not available to them when all else has failed?

Hearsay would have it that, at times, decisions regarding admissions may have been made with the needs of the centre more to the fore than the needs of children and young people with the innuendo being that staff and management wanted an 'easy life'. However, in my more than 20 years' experience in residential care across the statutory, voluntary and private sectors what I have most often witnessed is carefully evaluated and risk assessed decision-making on admissions based on the matching of the profile of the new admission to the existing residents, with priority being afforded to the needs of the existing residents. This, I am conscious, may have at times frustrated other professionals as they have the pressing, but singular, needs of their child to satisfy; a child who they are attempting to place in the residential centre within a national service where they are very limited and ever decreasing placements available. Whilst I may understand and appreciate their frustration and their motives for wanting the admission to proceed I would recommend that these professionals extend similar professional courtesy, respect and understanding to fellow professionals working in and managing what is a highly-regulated and professional service, children's residential care. We must, all of us, be wary of universalising the particular in social care.

Residential care is often left in a 'damned if you do and damned if you don't' situation in this regard. Damned if they admit the child inappropriately as the outcome will likely be poor and the service will be castigated for only achieving poor outcomes at great cost. Or if the child is not admitted the service is damned for being too selective and 'cherry picking' with the innuendo that it should be able to admit children when needed and manage the associated risks and challenges as that is what it is there for. In either scenario residential care is susceptible to being labelled as not working and wasteful, with waste identified as a cardinal sin in professional services publicly funded in the 21st century. Yet any professional tradesman knows that you must allow an excess, or waste, in calculations for materials such as tiles for flooring or wood for decking, or else you will fall short of material to accomplish the job as there is always wastage owing to irregular sizes of building and standard sizing of materials. Buildings are not built to uniform dimensions to accommodate materials, the materials are cut to fit the building; it is likewise with children and the supports they need. Consequently, there is a strong professional argument in favour of a certain amount of 'built-in-redundancy' (more resources than are strictly necessary to complete given tasks) for just these reasons within the social professions (Fenton, 2015). In reality, we all have a duty to care for all children in state care and we must work together in partnership rather than isolated professional silos.

Unfortunately, I have also witnessed some instances over the years where the admission process was not managed carefully enough and young people were inappropriately placed, albeit mostly with nothing but the best of intent on the part of all professionals involved. In these instances, the needs of these young people were not appropriately met in these centres and the placements of other children were also often disrupted. Good residential care can work well for children appropriately placed and these children may also benefit from appropriate and supportive peer relationships in such settings but equally they may be harmed in poorly configured and operated settings. The key is appropriate placement by carefully matching residents in a centre with a well-balanced and valued team operating with a coherent approach to care and supported to do so by all external stakeholders.

As the recent financial implosion of the Irish economy impacted on all aspects of Irish society cutbacks had a profoundly negative impact on children's services, both out-of-home and in-home services. I have witnessed an insidious growth in the lack of acceptance for the use of the word No. Historically, in my experience, the word No was always identified as a potential flash-point with regard to children in care but more recently I find that it is the care system itself that has become reactive and unaccepting of its usage. It does not align well with the 'more-for-less' philosophy, the mantra of austerity, so prevalent in today's Ireland and other neoliberally oppressed states.

Here residential child care is vulnerable as it is an expensive service to operate given staffing costs. However, specious rhetoric aside, the truth is that there is significantly less residential child care being provided in Ireland than there was fifteen years ago, with a lower percentage of children in care now placed in residential care than previously. Our numbers of children in care per capita are broadly similar, albeit slightly lower, to our neighbouring states. In 2012 the rate per 10,000 of population in Ireland was 5.4, in England 5.9 and Northern Ireland 6.1 (DCYA, 2016) whilst the usage of residential child care was at 5% of children in care in Ireland, and 8% in Northern Ireland (Fenton, 2015). In 2015 the usage of residential care in England was 12% (Narey, 2016).

A grave misunderstanding of the role of residential care is perpetuated by the referencing to the system of care (the full range of supports and services available to support children, young people and their families) as a spectrum or continuum of care. This locates residential care, as a placement of last resort, at one end of such a spectrum or continuum, with early intervention, family and community support at the other end. This, then, separates residential care from early intervention as polar opposites and casts residential care as only being valid when all preceding services have failed, thus reinforcing its status as a residualised service. This also identifies the elimination or minimisation of residential care as a positive reflection on the efficacy of the preceding support services on said spectrum or continuum with the converse also portrayed as holding true. These are very unhelpful misrepresentations of the role and potential of residential care as in reality residential care, correctly resourced and utilised, is a valid and indeed vital element of early intervention services.

However, some may say that I am exaggerating the residualisation of residential care and the misunderstanding of its place within early intervention services owing, perhaps, to personal bias or that I am poorly informed. Yes, I am biased after more than two decades working in residential care during which time I have witnessed its positive potential but this bias has not clouded my judgement, rather it affords me clarity in these matters derived from lived experience; and no I am not poorly informed. This is confirmed by the following statement made in response to a Parliamentary Question by the then Irish Minister for Children and Youth Affairs, James O'Reilly, in January 2016:

"There are a small number who, as the Deputy has acknowledged, are seriously challenging. Residential care is always the last option. *Of course, early intervention is a key part of addressing this, as are social supports for families who themselves (are) having difficulties parenting."* (Dáil Debate, 3212/16)

A key element of the concept of early intervention is to make the necessary supports available when first they are identified as required in order to prevent the escalation, entrenchment of harm or future trauma and therefore need for higher levels of support. Residential care will, for some, be required at this early point of intervention where targeted placements may successfully meet the needs of the children requiring this level of intervention and facilitate their return to a family placement thereafter (Ombudsman for Children, 2013). Early intervention without the option of residential care is not a robust service as a robust service requires access to all levels of supports to optimally function. So correctly valued, resourced and implemented residential care can be a proactive service which rather than being, as it is currently often portrayed as, a reactive service castigated as wasteful can, in fact, be highly cost-effective by preventively diminishing long-term costs. Residential child care has been negatively labelled, and we know the harm labelling can cause young people in social care, and to challenge this labelling we must cease making reference to the spectrum or continuum of care and instead reference the system of care; a dynamic, bi-directional system, rather than a linear system with fixed points.

We cannot resource early intervention, in its current format, at the expense of those currently in care, or requiring entry into care in the near future, via the dramatic reduction or elimination of residential care; these current needs must also be met, ideally in tandem with investing in early intervention services inclusive of residential care. Too often we see a lengthy gap in service provision with the closure of one service without an alternative available despite the significant financial savings achieved by these closures. The closure of High-Support Units in Ireland and the elimination of this entire service in 2014 is a prime example of such practices.

To further such insidious commercially-motivated agendas one strategy used to great effect under neoliberalism is the division of the sectors with the pitting of one sector against the other, for example the private against statutory or vice-versa. With regard to residential child care it is not the higher usage of private residential care provision now to the fore in Ireland that is responsible for the cost of provision of this service, a service which formerly was provided in higher quantities by the statutory sector and, at a minimum, at the same cost as the private sector (Fenton, 2015). It is the provision of this service that is responsible for this cost, regardless of what sector provides it. Professionals or politicians who espouse otherwise reveal their true agenda where careers can be advanced by the illusion of financial propriety. However, they do a grave disservice to those they are employed to assist; they weaken the system of care which impacts on all out-of-home services, including foster care, and condemn large numbers of children and young people to care biographies of multiple placement breakdowns which is known to be deleterious to their social, emotional and educational development. These children and young people have been brought into care with the promise that the state will do a better job of caring for them than those who were supposed to be caring for them previously yet the state fails them abjectly via such inadequate care. Is this not the ultimate hypocrisy where the state tells citizens how they should parent children but then cannot do this itself when needed? The state is better, though far from perfect, at being corporate than it is at being a parent.

If we genuinely care for all our children then we must provide the necessary services to meet the needs of those most traumatised and vulnerable of children who require adequate levels of well-resourced and valued residential care, including higher levels of support than mainstream care, within a well-developed range of placement options. To attempt to reduce even further a service that is already under-resourced, with insufficient availability to meet demand, is the ultimate expression of professional and moral negligence. No other state has sustainably reduced the levels of residential care beneath our current levels of 5%, with several European states currently providing more residential care than foster care and in this process achieving good outcomes (Fenton, 2015). Among the many reasons for these better outcomes is the fact that children are admitted younger into residential care and may remain in residential care for longer than children in Ireland or the UK. This practice maximises the benefits of placement in good quality residential care, that is not used as a placement of last resort but rather is valued and use appropriately, for these children (Narey, 2016). To think that clever 'demand-management' strategies and creative system and programme planning will achieve this is nothing but a deception or a delusion along the lines of those outlined in Richard Stivers (1999) in his insightful book "Technology as Magic".

The truth that is revealed when the layers of misunderstanding and misrepresentation are peeled back is that correctly utilised good-quality residential care, which encompasses catering for younger children, can be a positive option, rather than its current status as the placement of last resort after all else has failed, which failure then becomes attributed to residential care assigning it an identity as a negative option, a failure. In essence, it has become the scapegoat for the inefficacies of the care system.

It is indeed timely and welcome that the much anticipated independent report on residential child care in England, commissioned by David Cameron, has been published in July 2016 (Narey, 2016). This review was conducted by the highly respected former CEO of Barnardos and Government advisor Sir Martin Narey. The report supports much of what I have outlined above regarding residential child care and reinforces similar findings recently highlighted in a 2013 report by the Irish Ombudsman for Children (OCO, 2013).

"Children's homes are often viewed as an anachronism, to be used only as a last resort... The more that social workers and social work leaders of the future understand the potential of residential care, the less likely it will be treated as only something to be used as a last resort...I see very little scope for reducing our reliance on children's homes and I am quite clear that to do so would not be in the interests of children. As I have tried to make clear in this report, I think the role of children's homes is misunderstood, the challenge of the children they care for underestimated, and the contribution they make too easily dismissed." (Narey, 2016:5,9,69)

Given that Narey's report applies to a country with 12% usage of residential care for children in care it is clear that to target residential care in Ireland, with a current usage in 2016 of 5%, as an area where further money can be 'saved' takes little account of the needs of children.

As a frontline worker in residential care, I was conscious that I undertook this work partly to meet my own need to care, a need I was surprised to discover I possessed after many years in other work settings. This vocational calling is present in most care workers I encountered over the years albeit the nature of the need being met may differ. This affords our profession a bedrock of motivated staff few other occupations possess. I came to recognise this commonality of motivation, despite sometimes difference of opinion with my colleagues, as the glue that held our teams together through often difficult times. This motivation inspires the critical intentionality underpinning our actions which precludes task-orientated care practice whilst promoting the therapeutic aspects of care. This is our common ground.

> *"We do what we do because we care,*
> *and because we care,*
> *we do what we do to the best of our ability"*

To maximise the potential of this motivation it is imperative to empower workers to work relationally. One of the core challenges of residential care is to put in place the right circumstances for children and young people to succeed and similarly the challenge for those of us who no longer operate in frontline roles is to seek to setup the circumstances for workers to succeed. Workers need to be recognised for their commitment, dedication and skill and this requires that they have the time to spend *being with* children and nurturing meaningful relationships which promote the children's development rather than managing the children and record keeping. We must reclaim our profession and reinstate the relationship at its beating heart.

"We owe it to children – they need to know they are cared for by someone who is respected...Good care is not produced by tools – it's provided by people and investing in carers is investing in the heart and soul of children." (Anglin cited in Hillan, 2005:51)

Residential care is largely a dyadic exercise where what impacts on one party also impacts the other, i.e. worker and child. Therefore, we must promote healthy relationships at all levels of social care in order that the workers' role model these to the children having themselves experienced positive relationships with their leaders, managers and educators. I believe that it is a fundamental axiom that *"as we treat staff so they will treat the children"* and therefore supporting and valuing staff rather than seeking to maximise output from a perceived unit of resource assumes paramount significance. I also believe that the worker is themselves their most protective and empowering asset in their practice and therefore the use of self is critical to maximise this potential. Self-awareness, self-management and self-care, critical elements of emotional and professional competence

(Winter, 2009), are then critical to achieving this effective use of self; in other words, the workers' relationship with themselves, with others (professionals and young people) and also the systems within which they operate.

Systems which operate with sustained known unacceptable aberrations within their operation are dysfunctional systems as, by definition, aberrations are outside of the systems design specifications. In this context our current child care system which operates with unacceptable levels of violence directed towards staff (Keogh and Byrne, 2016) is then clearly dysfunctional. We are taught that all behaviour communicates a need and therefore such sustained levels of violent behaviour indicates that the needs of these children are not being met within the placement setting wherein they are currently being accommodated. The social ecology of residential child care has been excessively constricted in Ireland with predominately only mainstream residential care and a small number of special care places, (14 children were placed in Special Care in March 2016 (Tusla, 2016)), now attempting to cater for the welfare needs of all children in the state needing care. The needs of such a diverse group of children cannot be adequately, and therefore safely, met in a 'one-size fit all' model such as we currently have and we clearly need a range of specialist placements for children with higher levels of need, including mental health needs, than is currently available in Ireland. It is unacceptable that we continue to send extremely vulnerable children to foreign jurisdictions, (17 children in March 2016 (Tusla, 2016)), for their needs to be met when such services could be provided in this country.

Over my time working in residential care it has been my observation that the risks posed by the children and young people today have not become greater than was the case in the past, as is often alluded to with regard to violence and assault directed towards staff. Rather, I have observed that it is the systems within which workers operate, and children are cared for, that have changed, and, as highlighted above, with regard to diversity of placement options, for the poorer. Among the negative consequences here is that some children and young people have become reframed as the problems, unmanageable and dangerous. Inclusion in this grouping is all too easily accomplished by children whose needs are not being meet appropriately in care, when, in fact, it is the system itself which is the problem.

For the workers such dysfunctional systems place them at equal, if not in fact higher, risk of what can be described as 'system trauma' - that is to say trauma that is induced by working or being cared for within a deficient care system (Fenton, 2015:278) - than they are vulnerable to vicarious trauma from working with the children themselves. In fact, the positive potentials of vicarious resilience and compassion satisfaction can, once recognised and nurtured, counterbalance the negative potentials of vicarious trauma and compassion fatigue but the risk posed by system trauma cannot be mitigated other than by strengthening the system itself with a diverse range of well-resourced good-quality placement options. It is not more resilient workers alone that can ameliorate this risk of system trauma, as some imply, it is the system itself which must become more resilient within the context of a social ecology model of resilience.

As previously noted, *"One of the core challenges of residential care is to put in place the right circumstances for children in care to succeed and similarly the challenge for those of us who no longer operate in frontline roles is to seek to setup the circumstances for workers to succeed"* (Fenton, 2015:46). In this regard we can see that the task of staff creating the right circumstances for children to succeed is being hindered by the deficiencies within our current care system as identified above. The responsibility for this lies with those who commission, regulate, and oversee the development of residential care services nationally as well as the politicians who determine ideological approaches to, and budgets for, care provision. Both staff and children are at increased risk of harm as a result of these deficiencies.

Nothing succeeds like success and sometimes we, as staff faced with seemingly insurmountable obstacles and risks "have to fake it till we make it and encourage children and young people to do likewise" (Fenton, 2015). This is a strengths-based perspective where 'vicarious confidence' offered by staff can accentuate the positive that is within all children, albeit this may be suppressed by, for example, learned helplessness (Seligman, 1972; Weiner, 1986) and other consequences of adverse childhood events. However, our current care system focuses predominately on the negative, obsessed with risk as a negative construct to the exclusion of its intrinsic positive developmental potential, with residential care services that are under-resourced, under-valued and, immaturely, over regulated which, at times, further compounds the learned helplessness of the children. In the words of John Burton (2015):

"The social care sector is forced to prioritise the regulator's demands over the needs of its clients, and they really aren't the same."

To bring this section on relationship and residential care to a conclusion, we have seen that children's problems most often originate in their relationships with adults and therefore the only pathway to recovery is through positive relationships with appropriate adults. To use the language of commerce once more, *relationships* are the *currency* and *product* of social care.

As Gerry Fewster has said: 'The relationship *is* the intervention.'

Conclusion

So now it feels like time to bring to a conclusion what has developed from an initial brief email into what is now a small book outlining some of my core beliefs, curiosities and life experiences. The 'evidence' of my lived experience has taught me that my capacity to embrace my vulnerability is one of my most valuable assets in my practice as a social care professional and, somewhat counter-intuitively, I have come to recognise that what I had been socialised to regard as a weakness, vulnerability, has in fact often been both my most protective factor and greatest strength.

We all have our personal motivations for why we entered social care work and why so many leave and so few of us remain over the course of our working lives. It is certainly a most rewarding yet also demanding career. It is actions like writing this book and professional activism with other like-mined professionals coupled with a belief that it is better to try and fail than to fail to try, that are part of my self-care management in this ongoing process of advocating for and with children and young people in care as well as those people who state care has carelessly left, as for too many they do not leave care, care leaves them. It leaves them ill-prepared and alone, labelled by ignorance and assumption with their distress and pain too often condoned by societal and political indifference.

I close this short book with a quote from the diminutive yet inimitable Eileen Gambrill, (2013:x):

"*Understanding the relationships between the personal and the political will contribute to your courage as will inspiration drawn from others including clients who acted rather than remained passive in the face of injustice.*"

Bibliography

Alasuutari, P. Bickman, L. and Brannan, J. (2008). Introduction: Social Research in Changing Social Conditions. In Alasuutari, P. Bickman, L. and Brannan, J. (Eds.), *The Sage Handbook of Social Research Methods*, 1-8, London, Sage.

Anglin, J. (2004). Creating "Well-Functioning" Residential Care and defining Its Place in a System of Care, *Child & Youth Care Forum*, 33, 3, 75-192.

Arnett, J. (2007). Suffering, selfish, slackers? Myths and reality about emerging adults, *Journal of Youth and Adolescence*, 36, 23–9.

Bellefeuille, G. and Ricks, F. (2010). Relational Inquiry: A child and youth care approach to research, *Children and Youth Services Review*, 32, 1235-1241.

Bentley, K. (2005). Can there be any universal children's rights? *International Journal of Human Rights*, 9, 1, 107-123.

Bettleheim, B. (1975). *The Uses of Enchantment: The Meaning and Importance of Fairy Tales*, New York, Vintage Books.

Born, J. (2003). The emperor's clothes: Description of a new epidemic related to diagnostic imaging, *Acta Neurolgica Belgica*, 103, 140-143.

Burton, J. (2015). *After 50 years in the sector, I know the CQC rarely improves social care*, The Guardian, 22nd April.

Cashmore, J. and Paxman, M. (2006). Predicting after-care outcomes: the importance of 'felt' security, *Child and Family Social Work*, 11, 3, 232-241.

Coy, M. (2008). Young Women, Local Authority Care and Selling Sex, *British Journal of Social Work*, 38, 1408-1420.

Coy, M. (2009). Moved Around Like Bags of Rubbish Nobody Wants: How Multiple Placement Moves Can Make Young Women Vulnerable to Sexual Exploitation, *Child Abuse Review*, 18, 254-266.

Dáil Debates (3212/16). https://www.kildarestreet.com/debates/?id=2016-01-28a.126&s=childrens+residential+care#g131

Davis, M. & Vander Stoep, A. (1997). The transition to adulthood for youth who have serious emotional disturbance: developmental transition and young adult outcomes, *Journal of Mental Health Administration*, 24, 4, 400-427.

DCYA, (2016). http://www.dcya.gov.ie/viewdoc.asp?fn=/documents/Children_In_Care/ChildreninCareStatsandInterCompar.htm

Deming, D. (2015). *The Growing Importance of Social Skills in the Labor Market*, Harvard University and NBER.

http://scholar.harvard.edu/files/ddeming/files/deming_socialskills_august2015.pdf

Devine, T. (2004). *A study of ways a residential group care facility can foster resilience in adolescents who have experienced cumulative adversities.* Unpublished doctoral dissertation, Fielding Graduate Institute.

Dodge, K. Dishion, T. and Lansford, J. (Eds.) (2006). *Deviant Peer Influences in Programs for Youth, Problems and Solutions*, New York, Guildford Press.

Edmond, R. (2014).Longing to belong: children in residential care and their experiences of peer relationships at school and in the children's home, *Child & Family Social Work*, 9, 194-202.

Erikson, E. (1952). *Childhood and Society,* New York, Vintage.

Evetts, J. (2011). Sociological Analysis of Professionalism: Past, Present and Future, *Comparative Sociology*, 10, 1-37.

Fenton, M. (2014). *Unity through Relationship.* http://www.goodenoughcaring.com/the-journal/unity-through-relationship-2/

Fenton, M. (2015). *Social Care and Child Welfare in Ireland: Integrating Residential Care, Leaving Care and Aftercare,* Dublin, The Liffey Press.

Fenton, M. (2015a). *Doing The Right Thing for Children in Care and Support Seekers*.http://www.goodenoughcaring. com/the-journal/doing-the-right-thing-for-children-in-care-and-support-seekers/

Ferguson, H. (2007). Abused and Looked After Children as 'Moral Dirt': Child Abuse and Institutional Care in Historical Perspective, *Journal of Social Policy,* 36, 1, 123-139.

Freud, S. (1939). *Moses and monotheism, S. E* (Vol. 23), New York, Basic Book.

Furnivall, J. McKenna, M, McFarlane, S. & Grant, E. (2012). *Attachment Matters for All – An Attachment Mapping Exercise for Children's Services in Scotland*, Scotland, CELCIS.

http://www.celcis.org/media/resources/publications/ Attachment-Matters-For-All.pdf

Gambrill, E. (2013). *Social Work Practice: A Critical Thinkers Guide*, 3rd Ed., New York, Oxford University Press.

Garfat, T. (2003). *Four parts magic: The anatomy of a Child and Youth Care intervention.*

http://www.cyc-net.org/cyc-online/cycol-0303-thom.html

Giddens, A. (1991). *Modernity and Self-Identity. Self and Society in the Late Modern Age,* Cambridge, Polity.

Goleman, D. (1996). *Emotional Intelligence: Why it Can Matter More ThanIQ,* London, Bloomsbury.

Hawley, D.R. (2000), 'Clinical implications of family resilience', *American Journal of Family Therapy,* 28, 2, 101–116.

Hillan, L. (2005). *Reclaiming Residential Care: A Positive Choice for Children and Young People in Care,* The Winston Churchill Memorial Trust of Australia.

http://www.acwa.asn.au/cafwaa/Churchill_Report_Lisa_Hillan_2006.pdf

Hollis, J.(2005). Convergent Patterns in Jung and Yeats, *Psychological Perspectives: A Quarterly Journal of Jungian Thought,* 48, 2, 288-297.

Holohan, C. (2011). *In Plain Sight: Responding to the Ferns, Ryan, Murphy and Cloyne Reports,* Dublin, Amnesty.

Howe, D. (1998). Relationship based thinking and practice in social work, *Journal of Social Work Practice,* 12, 45-56.

Howe, D. (2008). *The Emotionally Intelligent Social Worker,* Basingstoke, Palgrave Macmillan.

Ingram, R. (2013). Locating Emotional Intelligence at the Heart of Social Work Practice, *British Journal of Social Work,* 43, 987-1004.

Keogh, V. and Byrne, C. (2016). *Crisis, Concern and Complacency; A study on the extent, impact and management of workplace violence and assault on social care workers*, Dublin, Social Care Ireland.

Kinnvall, C. (2004). Globalization and Religious Nationalism: Self, Identity, and the Search for Ontological Security, *Political Psychology*, 25, 5, 741-767.

Kuhn, T. (1962). *The Structure of Scientific Revolutions*, Chicago, University of Chicago Press.

Laing, R.D. (1973). *The Divided Self*, Harmondsworth, Penguin Books Ltd.

Lansdown, G. (2005). *The Evolving Capacities of the Child*, Innocenti Insight, UNICEF.

Li, J. & Julian, M. (2012). Developmental Relationships as the Active Ingredient: A Unifying Working Hypothesis of "What Works" Across Intervention Settings, *American Journal of Orthopsychiatry*, 82, 2, 157-166.

Little, M. Kohm, A. and Thompson, R. (2005). The impact of residential placement on child development: research and policy implications, *International Journal of Social Welfare*, 14, 3, 200-209.

Masten, A. (2015). *Ordinary magic: Resilience in development*, Guilford Press, London.

Meihuizen, N. (1992). Yeats, Jung and the Integration of Archetypes, *Theoria: A Journal of Social and Political Theory*, 80, 101-116.

Melrose, M. and Pearce, J. (2013). *Critical Perspectives on Child Sexual Exploitation and Related Trafficking*, Basingstoke, Palgrave Macmillan.

Morrison, T. (2007). Emotional intelligence, emotion and social work: context, characteristics, complications and contribution, *British Journal of Social Work*, 37, 245–263.

Munro, E. (2011). *The Munro Review of Child Protection: Final Report. A child-centred system*, London, Department of Education.

www.education.gov.uk/publications/eOrderingDownload/Munro-Review.pdf

Nadjiwan, H. (2010). Restorative Justice in Education: Monthly Dialogue, 1, 8, 1-2.http://shalemnetwork.org/wp-content/uploads/2011/12/RJ-MONTHLY-June-10.pdf

Narey, M. (2016). *Residential Care in England.*

https://www.gov.uk/government/uploads/system/uploads/attachment_data/file/534560/Residential-Care-in-England-Sir-Martin-Narey-July-2016.pdf

Neff, K. (2015). *The Self-Compassion Scale is a Valid and Theoretically Coherent Measure of Self-Compassion,* http://self-compassion.org/wp-content/uploads/2015/12/ScaleMindfulness.pdf

Noddings, N. (1996). *Caring: A Feminine Approach to Ethics and Moral Education*, Berkeley, University of California.

O'Leary, P. Tsui, M. & Ruch, G. (2013). The Boundaries of the Social Work Relationship Revisited: Towards a Connected, Inclusive and Dynamic Conceptualisation, *British Journal of Social Work*, 43, 1, 135-153.

Obholzer, A. and Roberts, V. (1994). *The Unconscious at Work: Individual and Organisational Stress in the Human Services,* Hove, Routledge.

Olney, J. (1992). *The Rhizome and the Flower: The Perennial Philosophy – Yeats and Jung,* University of California Press.

Ombudsman for Children (OCO), (2013). *A Meta Analysis of Repetitive Root Cause Issues Regarding the Provision of Services for Children in Care.* http://www.oco.ie/wp-content/uploads/2014/03/OCOMeta-analysisofservicesforchildrenincare.pdf

Rogers, C. (1965).*The Concept of the Fully Functioning Person*, Pastoral Psychology, 16, 3, 21-33. http://link.springer.com/article/10.1007%2FBF01769775

Rose, R. (2012). *Life Story Therapy with Traumatized Children: A Model for Practice,* London, Jessica Kingsley Publications.

Rovelli, C. (2014). *Science Is Not About Certainty.* https://newrepublic.com/article/118655/theoretical-phyisicist-explains-why-science-not-about-certainty

Rutter, M. (1999). Resilience concepts and findings: implications for family therapy, *The Journal of Family Therapy,* 21, 119-144.

Salovey, P. and Mayer, J. (1990). Emotional Intelligence, University of New Hampshire. http://www.unh.edu/emotional_intelligence/EIAssets/EmotionalIntelligenceProper/EI1990%20Emotional%20Intelligence.pdf

Schofiled, G. Larsson, B. and Ward, E. (2016). Risk, resilience and identity construction in the life narratives of young people leaving residential care, *Child & Family Social Work,* doi: 10.1111/cfs.12295.

Schneider, T. Lyons, J. and Khazon, S. (2013). Emotional Intelligence and Resilience, *Personality and Individual Differences,* 55, 8, 909-914.

Sehgal, P. (2015). *The Profound Emptiness of 'Resilience',* New York Times Magazine.

http://www.nytimes.com/2015/12/06/magazine/the-profound-emptiness-of-resilience.html?_r=0

Seligman, M. (1972). Learned helplessness, *Annual Review of Medicine*, 23, 1, 407–412.

Shulman, L. (1999). *The Skills of Helping Individuals, Families, Groups and Communities*, Illinois, Peacock.

Smith, M. (2009). *Rethinking Residential Childcare: Positive Perspectives*, Bristol, Policy Press.

Snow, P. (2014). *Yeats "Magic" is Jung's Science.*

https://uncertaintist.wordpress.com/2014/04/03/yeats-magic-is-jungs-science/

Stein, M. (2012). *Young People Leaving Care: Supporting Pathways to Adulthood,* London, Jessica Kingsley.

Stivers, R. (1999). *Technology as Magic: The Triumph of the Irrational*, New York, Continuum.

Stoltz, P. (1997). *Adversity quotient: Turning obstacles into opportunities*, New York, Wiley. http://www.peaklearning.com

T2A, (2015). Stolen Lives and Missed Opportunities: The deaths of young adults and children in prison. http://www.barrowcadbury.org.uk/wp-content/uploads/2015/02/Inquest-Report_finalversion_Online.pdf

Tam, H. (1998). *Communitarianism: A New Agenda for Politics and Citizenship*, Basingstoke, Macmillan Press.

Thompson, N. (2015). *The Authentic Leader*, Basingstoke, Palgrave Macmillan.

Trevithick, P. (2003). Effective relationship-based practice: a theoretical exploration, *Journal of Social Work Practice*, 17, 2, 163-176.

Trevithick, P. (2014). Humanising Managerialism: Reclaiming Emotional Reasoning, Intuition, the Relationship, and knowledge and Skills in Social Work, *Journal of Social Work Practice*, 28, 3, 287-311.

Tusla, (2016). Integrated Performance and Activity Report, Quarter 1.
http://www.tusla.ie/uploads/content/Q1_2016_Integrated_Performance_and_Activity_Report_Final.pdf

Ungar, M. (Ed.) (2012). *The Social Ecology of Resilience: A Handbook*, New York, Springer.

University of East Anglia. *Study explores emotional intelligence and stress in social work*, ScienceDaily.
www.sciencedaily.com/releases/2016/06/160627214253.htm

Van Rooy, D. and Viswesvaran, C. (2004). Emotional intelligence: a meta-analytic investigation of predictive validity and nomological net, *Journal of Vocational Behavior*, 65, 71–95.

Vaswani, N. (2014). The ripples of death: Exploring the bereavement experiences and mental health of young men in custody, *The Howard Journal of Criminal Justice*, 53, 4, 341–359.

Weiner, B. (1986). *An attributional theory of motivation and emotion*, New York, Springer-Verlag.

Whittaker, J. del Valle, J. and Holmes, L. (2015). *Therapeutic Residential Care for Children and Youth*, London, Jessica Kingsley Publishers.

Winnicott, D. Winnicott, C. Shepherd, R. and Davis, M. (1984). *Deprivation and Delinquency*, London, Tavistock Publications.

Winter, K. (2009). Relationships matter: the problems and prospects for social workers' relationships with young children in care, *Child and Family Social Work*, 14, 450-460.

Yeats, W. (1901). Magic, *The Monthly Review* (London), 4, 12, 144-162.

Index